GO FACTS Physical science

Simple Machines

A & C BLACK • LONDON

Simple Machines

© 2007 Blake Publishing
Additional Material © A & C Black Publishers Ltd 2008

First published in 2007 in Australia by Blake Education Pty Ltd.

This edition published 2008 in the United Kingdom by
A & C Black Publishers Ltd, 38 Soho Square, London W1D 3HB.

Hardback edition
ISBN 9781408102619

Paperback edition
ISBN 9781408104774

A CIP record for this book is available from the British Library.

Author: Ian Rohr
Publishers: Katy Pike
Editor: Mark Stafford
Design and layout by The Modern Art Production Group

Image credits: cover (main image) Shutterstock; p9 (top)–US Navy photo by Sam
Shore; p13 (all)–Mark Stafford

Printed in China by WKT Company Ltd.

This book is produced using paper that is made from wood grown in
managed sustainable forests. It is natural, renewable and recyclable.
The logging and manufacturing processes conform to the environmental
regulations of the country of origin.

contents

What is a Simple Machine?

A machine is a tool that makes work easier. A simple machine is a simple tool.

Work occurs when a **force** makes something move. Lifting a heavy box out of a lorry requires work. It needs a lifting force. The job is easier if you slide the box down a ramp. A ramp is a simple machine.

A simple machine does not reduce the amount of work needed to do something, but it can spread the force over a longer distance. This makes the work easier. It can also change the direction or speed of a force.

A simple machine has only a few moving parts. Some simple machines have no moving parts.

There are two main types of simple machines – inclined planes and levers. Ramps, screws and wedges are types of inclined planes. Pulleys, wheels and axles are types of levers.

We use things every day that are simple machines. Opening a door, turning on a tap and even walking up stairs uses simple machines.

wheel and axle

wedge

All these activities rely on simple machines.

screw

pulley

ramp

Inclined Planes

An inclined plane is a flat surface with one end higher than the other.

An inclined plane is one of the simplest kinds of machines. If you use an inclined plane to raise something, you don't need as much force as if you lift it straight up.

The steeper the slope of the inclined plane, the greater the force needed to push an object up it. The flatter the slope, the less force needed to push something up it, but you have to push further to get to the same height.

Stairs and sloped paths are inclined planes. It is easier to walk up a long, gentle hill than to climb up a short, steep hill.

Escalators, boat ramps, ski jumps and ladders are all inclined planes.

It is easier to walk up stairs than climb straight up.

The Ancient Egyptians used ramps to build the Great Pyramid of Giza.

Winding roads over a mountain are inclined planes. Cars travel further to get to the top.

7

Wedges

single wedge

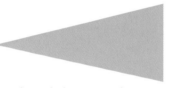

double wedge

A wedge changes the direction of a force.

When a force pushes down on a wedge, the wedge makes the push force go out in two directions.

A single wedge looks like an inclined plane. It has one sloping surface.
A doorstop is a single wedge. It pushes the door and floor apart.

A double wedge has two inclined planes, back to back. It has two sloping surfaces.
The head of an axe is a double wedge.

The force used to swing an axe becomes greater when it splits wood.

A kitchen knife is a double wedge. Its cutting power depends on how sharp and thick it is.

A nail is also a wedge. The sharp tip of the nail pushes wood apart. This makes it easier to hammer the nail in.

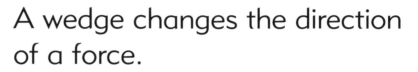

Your sharp, front teeth are wedges.

The bow of a boat is a wedge. It divides water.

A cutting edge is a wedge.

GO FACT!

THE FASTEST

A woodchopper can chop through a log 30 centimetres thick in eight seconds.

9

Levers

Levers lift or move loads. They are one of the most common simple machines. Almost every object with a handle acts as a lever.

A lever is a stiff bar or board that rests on a point. The bar or board turns on the point. This point is called a **fulcrum**.

If you push or pull on one end of the lever, you apply a force. The other end of the lever goes in the opposite direction. The object that a lever moves is called the **load**.

A hammer is a first class lever when it is used to pull out a nail.

The closer the fulcrum is to the load, the less force is needed to lift the load. The load moves a shorter distance than the push or pull force.

The closer the fulcrum is to the force, the greater the force is needed to lift the load. The load moves a greater distance than the push or pull force.

There are three classes of lever. The class depends on the positions of the fulcrum, load and force.

class of lever	examples
first class the fulcrum is between the force and the load	
second class the fulcrum is at one end, the force at the other, and the load is in the middle	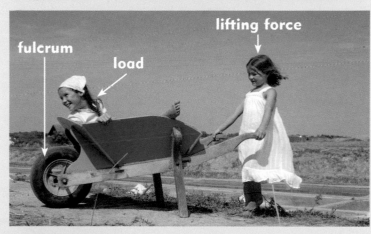
third class the fulcrum is at one end, and the force is between the fulcrum and the load	

Working with Levers

What's the easiest way to break a toothpick or crack a nut?

What you need:

- two toothpicks
- a nutcracker
- a hard nut

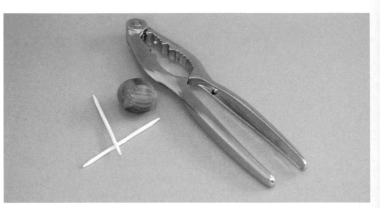

1 Place a toothpick across the back of your middle finger, just behind your finger nail. It should go under your first and third fingers. Try to break the toothpick by pressing down with your first and third fingers.

2 Move the toothpick closer to your knuckle. Try again to break the toothpick with your fingers. The fulcrum is your knuckle.

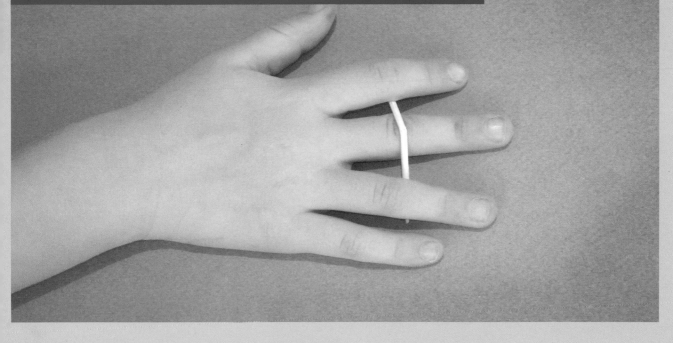

3 Now, try to crack a nut with a nutcracker. Start by placing the nut at the far end of the nutcracker, nearest your hands. Then move the nut closer to the joint of the nutcracker, which is the fulcrum.

The further away the toothpick and nut are from the fulcrum, the more force is needed to break them.

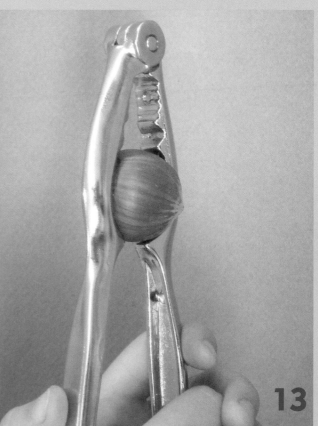

Pulleys

A pulley uses a wheel and a rope to raise or lower a load. It increases a force or changes its direction.

A simple pulley has one wheel. The rope runs through a groove on the wheel. One end of the rope is tied to a load, and a force pulls on the other end. Simple pulleys are used on blinds and sailing boats.

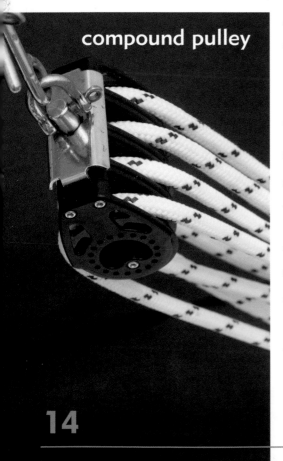

compound pulley

A rope can run through more than one pulley. With two pulleys, only half the force is needed to lift a load. The rope has to be pulled twice as far. With three pulleys, only one third of the force is needed, and the rope needs to be pulled three times as far.

A **compound** pulley has more than one wheel. It is also called a **block and tackle**. The more sections of rope used, the easier it is to move the load.

pull down the rope

flags go up

A pulley can change the direction of a force.

Ropes and pulleys can help one person lift another.

GO FACT!

THE TALLEST

The tallest flag pole in the world is at Panmunjon, North Korea. It is 160 metres high and flies a flag 30 metres long.

A crane using pulleys can lift almost anything.

Screws

Screws hold things together, and lower and raise things.

A screw is an inclined plane wrapped around a **cylinder**. The inclined plane forms a ridge along the cylinder. This ridge is called the **thread** of the screw.

As a screw is turned by a screwdriver, it turns a greater distance than it moves forwards. The turning motion becomes a forwards motion.

A Greek **mathematician** called Archimedes invented a screw machine more than 1,200 years ago. It was used to lift water. The machine was a long screw inside a pipe. One end sat in the water. As the machine was turned, water was scooped into the turning thread and carried to the top of the screw. It then flowed out of a hole at the top. The screw machine was used to lift water into fields and out of ships.

The screw in a vice allows it to be closed very tightly.

The closer together the threads, the easier it is to turn the screw.

A spiral staircase is a screw. It is easier to climb one than to walk up a straight staircase.

THE LARGEST

A propeller is a type of screw. It provides a push force. The world's largest ship propeller is 9.1 metres high – as tall as a three storey building. It has six blades and is turned by the world's most powerful diesel engine.

This screw crushes grapes.

17

Wheels and Axles

A wheel with a rod called an axle through its centre can lift and move loads.

The axle is joined to the wheel. When either the wheel or axle turns, the other part also turns. The steering wheel in a car is a wheel and axle.

The circle turned by the wheel is much larger than the circle turned by the axle. The longer distance turned by the wheel makes the axle turn more powerfully.

A wheel and axle is often used with **gears**. A gear is a wheel with **cogs** around its edge. Several gears can be connected, so that their cogs lock into each other. The gears can be different sizes. When one gear turns, it makes the other gears turn.

A door knob is a simple wheel and axle.

If one gear turned, which way would the others turn?

A bicycle has different sized gears.

wheel →

axle →

THE LARGEST
A Ferris wheel is a large wheel and axle. The largest Ferris wheel in the world is the London Eye, but bigger ones are being built in Asia.

19

Compound Machines

Many of the machines we use every day are compound machines.

A **compound machine** is made from two or more simple machines working together as one.

A spade is a compound machine. The handle is a lever, and the blade is a wedge. A can-opener is made up of levers, a wedge and a wheel and axle. Even complex machines, such as cars or areoplanes, are based on the six simple machines.

All the things on these pages are compound machines.

lever

wheel and axle

wedge

lever

wheel and axle

lever

screw

screw

lever

lever

lever

pulley

wheel and axle

21

Simple Machines at Work

Inclined plane			
Wedge			
Lever			
Pulley			
Screw			
Wheel and Axle			

Glossary

block and tackle	a compound pulley (the block) and the ropes attached to it (the tackle)
cog	a tooth on the edge of a gear
compound	made of two or more parts
compound machine	two or more simple machines working as one machine
cylinder	a tube with long straight sides and two circular ends
force	a push or pull that changes the speed, direction or shape of something
fulcrum	the point on which a lever turns
gear	a wheel with teeth around the edge that connects to other gears
load	the weight to be moved or supported
mathematician	someone who is an expert in mathematics
thread	a ridge that goes around the outside of a screw

Index